ω 10/13 ω 4/16

FE -- 12

⟨DK⟩ READERS

Level 1

A Note to Parents

DK READERS is a compelling program for beginning readers, designed in conjunction with leading literacy experts, including Dr. Linda Gambrell, Distinguished Professor of Education at Clemson University. Dr. Gambrell has served as President of the National Reading Conference, the College Reading Association, and the International Reading Association.

Beautiful illustrations and superb full-color photographs combine with engaging, easy-to-read stories to offer a fresh approach to each subject in the series. Each DK READER is guaranteed to capture a child's interest while developing his or her reading skills, general knowledge, and love of reading.

The five levels of DK READERS are aimed at different reading abilities, enabling you to choose the books that are exactly right for your child:

Pre-level 1: Learning to read
Level 1: Beginning to read
Level 2: Beginning to read alone
Level 3: Reading alone
Level 4: Proficient readers

The "normal" age at which a child begins to read can be anywhere from three to eight years old. Adult participation through the lower levels is very helpful for providing encouragement, discussing storylines, and sounding out unfamiliar words.

No matter which level you select, you can be sure that you are helping your child learn to read, then read to learn!

LONDON, NEW YORK, MUNICH,
MELBOURNE, AND DELHI

Editor Dawn Sirett
Art Editor Jane Horne
Series Editor Deborah Lock
Managing Art Editor Martin Wilson
US Editor Regina Kahney
Production Editor Sarah Isle
Picture Researcher Angela Anderson
Jacket Designer Natalie Godwin
Natural History Consultant
Theresa Greenaway

Reading Consultant
Linda B. Gambrell, Ph.D.

First American Edition, 2000
This edition, 2012
12, 13, 14, 15 16 10 9 8 7 6 5 4 3 2 1
Published in the United States by DK Publishing
375 Hudson Street, New York, New York 10014

Published in Great Britain by Dorling Kindersley Limited.
DK books are available at special discounts when purchased in bulk
for sales promotions, premiums, fund-raising, or educational use.
For details, contact: DK Publishing Special Markets
375 Hudson Street, New York, New York 10014
SpecialSales@dk.com

A catalog record for this book is available
from the Library of Congress

ISBN: 978-0-7566-9087-8 (pb)
ISBN: 978-0-7566-9086-1 (plc)

Color reproduction by Colourscan, Singapore
Printed and bound in China by L Rex Printing Co., Ltd.

The publisher would like to thank the following for
their kind permission to reproduce their photographs:
Key: a=above, c=center, b=below, l=left, r=right, t=top
Ardea London Ltd: Peter Steyn 4 bl; **Bruce Coleman Collection Ltd**:
Trevor Barrett 6–7, 19 c, Erwin & Peggy Bauer 28,
Fred Bruemmer 10 t, Alain Compost front cover, 17,
Peter Davey 26 b, Chrisler Fredriksson 27 cl, 32 crb, Janos Jurka 22 t,
Steven C. Kaufman 15 t, 15 cr, 32 bl, Gunter Kohler 16 c,
Stephen Krasemann 24 b, Leonard Lee 7 t, Joe McDonald 3 b, 23 b,
M. R. Phicton 4 cra, 4 cr, Jorg & Petra Wegner 5 b; **NHPA**: B. & C.
Alexander 12 b; **Oxford Scientific Films**: Martyn Colbeck 9 t, 30–31 b,
Daniel J. Cox 14 tr, 14–15 b, 32 clb, Kenneth Day 5 tr, 13 t, 32 tl,
Michael Fogden 13 b, Zig Leszczynski 10 b;
Planet Earth Pictures: Gary Bell 29 c, 29 inset, 32 br, Tom Brakefield 21 t,
Robert Franz 25, M. & C. Denis Huot 2 br, 18 b, Brian Kenney 27 t,
Pavlo de Oliveira 8–9 b, Doug Perrine 20–21 b.

Additional photography for DK: Peter Anderson, Jane Burton,
Frank Greenaway, Colin Keates, Dave King, Bill Ling, and Tim Ridley.
Jacket images: Front: FLPA: Donald M. Jones / Minden Pictures.
All other images © Dorling Kindersley Limited
For further information see: www.dkimages.com

Discover more at
www.dk.com

DK READERS

BEGINNING
1
TO READ

Wild
Baby Animals

Written by Karen Wallace

DK Publishing

Animals grow up in different ways.
They have lots of lessons to learn.
Some are born helpless,
but their mothers protect them.
A newborn kangaroo is the size
of a bee.

She crawls
into her
mother's
safe pouch.

She doesn't open her eyes
for at least five months.

A newborn monkey cannot walk.
He is carried by his mother.

Other baby animals
can walk soon after they're born.
They learn to run
with their mother
when danger is near.

Baby rhinos stand on their hooves
a few minutes after
they are born.

hooves

A baby zebra can run
an hour after she is born.

Some baby animals are born
in a place that is safe.
Other baby animals are born
in the open.

Baby wolves are born in a cave.

A baby elephant is born on open, grassy land.

Other elephants make a circle to protect her.

All the animals in this book
drink their mother's milk.
They are called mammals.

A seal's milk is fatty and rich.
Baby seals need lots of fat
to keep warm in the snow.

Baby bears
suck milk
for six months.

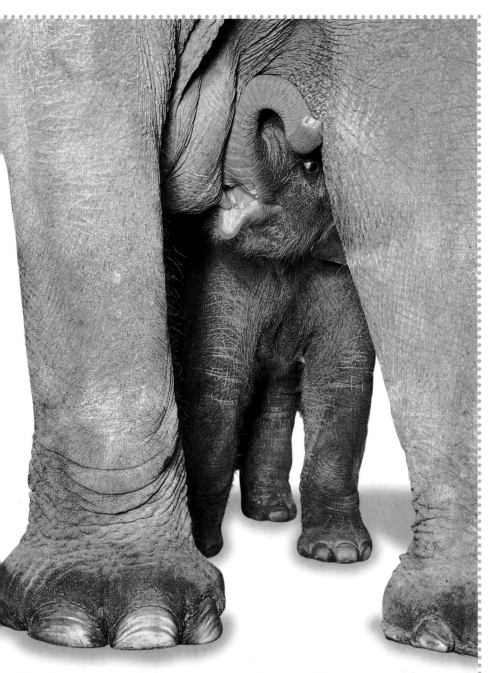

Baby elephants suck milk
for two years or more!

All baby mammals
stay by their mother
to keep safe.

On land, a baby walrus
stays tucked under her mother.

A baby kangaroo is carried
in his mother's pouch.

A baby sloth has to hold on tight.
Her mother is upside down!

Baby animals
must stay clean
to be healthy.

tongue

A mother cheetah licks
her cub's soft fur with
her rough tongue.

A monkey picks lice
from her baby's back
with her long fingers.

As baby animals grow
they need solid food.

Lion cubs eat
what their mother can catch.

Baby orangutans
eat fruit
that their mother
has chewed for them.

Other baby animals
soon find food for themselves.
A baby buffalo eats grass.

A baby giraffe tears off leaves
with her thick lips.

Baby animals
know their mother's voice.
They find her quickly
if danger is near.

A baby dolphin
hears her mother
make a click-click-click sound.

CLICK!
CLICK!
CLICK!

A baby seal
knows her mother's bark. *ARRK!*

When there's danger in the water, baby animals do as they're told.

Baby beavers dive when they hear the whack of their mother's tail.

tail

A baby hippo
stays with his mother
when she grunts a loud warning.

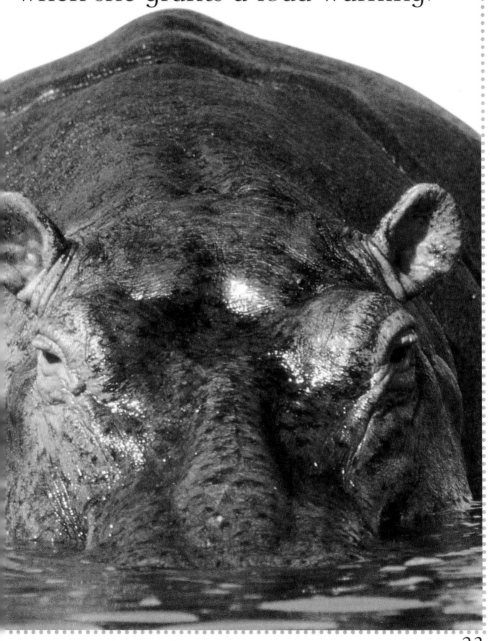

When there's danger
in the forest,
baby animals do as they're told.

A fawn lies still
in the grass
so she won't be seen.

Bear cubs
climb a tree
when their
mother growls.

As baby animals grow older
they start
to look after themselves.

A young chimpanzee
uses a stick to dig for insects.

Otter cubs learn to swim so they can catch fish.

A young elephant uses her trunk to rip leaves from a tree.

trunk

Baby animals play games
that teach them how
to look after themselves.

Wolf cubs wrestle and bite.
They're pretending to hunt.

Baby koalas play in the trees.
They're learning to climb
with their sharp claws.

claws

Baby animals grow up.
They learn their lessons well
and no longer need
their mothers.

Koalas are
fully grown
at two years.

Elephants are
fully grown
at twenty-five!

One day baby animals
are old enough
to have babies of their own.

Glossary

Claws
sharp nails on the end of an animal's hand or toes

Hooves
a horned covering over the foot of an animal

Tail
a movable body part joined to an animal's bottom

Tongue
a fleshy part in the mouth used for tasting and eating

Trunk
the long nose of an elephant

Index